MAD LIBS®

HAPPILY EVER MAD LIBS

By Roger Price and Leonard Stern

PSS!
PRICE STERN SLOAN
An Imprint of Penguin Group (USA) Inc.

PRICE STERN SLOAN
Published by the Penguin Group
Penguin Group (USA) Inc., 375 Hudson Street, New York, New York 10014, USA
Penguin Group (Canada), 90 Eglinton Avenue East, Suite 700, Toronto, Ontario M4P 2Y3, Canada
(a division of Pearson Penguin Canada Inc.)
Penguin Books Ltd., 80 Strand, London WC2R 0RL, England
Penguin Group Ireland, 25 St. Stephen's Green, Dublin 2, Ireland
(a division of Penguin Books Ltd.)
Penguin Group (Australia), 250 Camberwell Road, Camberwell, Victoria 3124, Australia
(a division of Pearson Australia Group Pty. Ltd.)
Penguin Books India Pvt. Ltd.,
11 Community Centre, Panchsheel Park, New Delhi—110 017, India
Penguin Group (NZ), 67 Apollo Drive, Rosedale, North Shore 0632, New Zealand
(a division of Pearson New Zealand Ltd.)
Penguin Books (South Africa) (Pty.) Ltd., 24 Sturdee Avenue,
Rosebank, Johannesburg 2196, South Africa

Penguin Books Ltd., Registered Offices: 80 Strand, London WC2R 0RL, England

Mad Libs format copyright © 2010 by Price Stern Sloan.

Published by Price Stern Sloan,
a division of Penguin Young Readers Group,
345 Hudson Street, New York, New York 10014.

ISBN 978-0-8431-9962-8

9 10

MAD LIBS
INSTRUCTIONS

MAD LIBS® is a game for people who don't like games!
It can be played by one, two, three, four, or forty.

• RIDICULOUSLY SIMPLE DIRECTIONS

In this tablet you will find stories containing blank spaces where words
are left out. One player, the READER, selects one of these stories. The
READER does not tell anyone what the story is about. Instead, he/she asks
the other players, the WRITERS, to give him/her words. These words are
used to fill in the blank spaces in the story.

• TO PLAY

The READER asks each WRITER in turn to call out a word—an adjective or
a noun or whatever the space calls for—and uses them to fill in the blank
spaces in the story. The result is a MAD LIBS® game.

When the READER then reads the completed MAD LIBS® game to the other
players, they will discover that they have written a story that is fantastic,
screamingly funny, shocking, silly, crazy, or just plain dumb—depending
upon which words each WRITER called out.

• EXAMPLE (*Before* and *After*)

"_____ !" he said _____
                  EXCLAMATION   ADVERB

as he jumped into his convertible _____ and
                                                    NOUN

drove off with his _____ wife.
                         ADJECTIVE

"_____*Ouch*_____ !" he said _____*Stupidly*_____
         EXCLAMATION   ADVERB

as he jumped into his convertible _____*cat*_____ and
                                              NOUN

drove off with his _____*brave*_____ wife.
                         ADJECTIVE

In case you have forgotten what adjectives, adverbs, nouns, and verbs are, here is a quick review:

An ADJECTIVE describes something or somebody. *Lumpy*, *soft*, *ugly*, *messy*, and *short* are adjectives.

An ADVERB tells how something is done. It modifies a verb and usually ends in "ly." *Modestly*, *stupidly*, *greedily*, and *carefully* are adverbs.

A NOUN is the name of a person, place, or thing. *Sidewalk*, *umbrella*, *bridle*, *bathtub*, and *nose* are nouns.

A VERB is an action word. *Run*, *pitch*, *jump*, and *swim* are verbs. Put the verbs in past tense if the directions say PAST TENSE. *Ran*, *pitched*, *jumped*, and *swam* are verbs in the past tense.

When we ask for A PLACE, we mean any sort of place: a country or city (*Spain*, *Cleveland*) or a room (*bathroom*, *kitchen*).

An EXCLAMATION or SILLY WORD is any sort of funny sound, gasp, grunt, or outcry, like *Wow!*, *Ouch!*, *Whomp!*, *Ick!*, and *Gadzooks!*

When we ask for specific words, like a NUMBER, a COLOR, an ANIMAL, or a PART OF THE BODY, we mean a word that is one of those things, like *seven*, *blue*, *horse*, or *head*.

When we ask for a PLURAL, it means more than one. For example, *cat* pluralized is *cats*.

MAD LIBS® is fun to play with friends, but you can also play it by yourself! To begin with, DO NOT look at the story on the page below. Fill in the blanks on this page with the words called for. Then, using the words you have selected, fill in the blank spaces in the story.

Now you've created your own hilarious MAD LIBS® game!

JACK AND THE BEANSTALK

NOUN _____

NOUN _____

PERSON IN ROOM _____

PLURAL NOUN_____

ADJECTIVE _____

NOUN _____

PART OF THE BODY (PLURAL) _____

ADJECTIVE _____

ADJECTIVE _____

SILLY WORD _____

PLURAL NOUN_____

NUMBER _____

MAD LIBS®

JACK AND THE BEANSTALK

Once upon a time there was a/an _____ named Jack
                                         NOUN

who lived with his mother in a tiny _____. The only
                                              NOUN

thing they owned was a cow named _____. Jack's mom
                                          PERSON IN ROOM

told him to sell the cow to buy some _____. On his way
                                            PLURAL NOUN

to the market, Jack met a stranger who said, "I'll trade you these

_____ beans for your cow." Jack agreed, but when his mom
      ADJECTIVE

learned he had disobeyed her, she was angrier than a wild

_____ and threw the beans out the window. As they slept,
      NOUN

the beans grew into a gigantic beanstalk. When Jack awoke, he

couldn't believe his _____. He immediately
                          PART OF THE BODY (PLURAL)

climbed the _____ beanstalk. At the top, he met a/an
                   ADJECTIVE

_____ giant. "Fee, fi, fo, _____!" the angry
      ADJECTIVE   SILLY WORD

giant bellowed. Jack quickly escaped, grabbing a hen that laid golden

_____, and quickly climbed down the beanstalk. With
      PLURAL NOUN

their newfound wealth, Jack and his mother bought _____
                                                              NUMBER

cows and lived happily ever after.

From HAPPILY EVER MAD LIBS®. Copyright © 2010 by Price Stern Sloan,
a division of Penguin Young Readers Group, 345 Hudson Street, New York, NY 10014.

MAD LIBS® is fun to play with friends, but you can also play it by yourself! To begin with, DO NOT look at the story on the page below. Fill in the blanks on this page with the words called for. Then, using the words you have selected, fill in the blank spaces in the story.

Now you've created your own hilarious MAD LIBS® game!

LIVE WITH HANSEL AND GRETEL

ADJECTIVE _____

PLURAL NOUN _____

ADJECTIVE _____

ADJECTIVE _____

PLURAL NOUN _____

PLURAL NOUN _____

ADJECTIVE _____

NOUN _____

PLURAL NOUN _____

NOUN _____

ADJECTIVE _____

CELEBRITY _____

MAD LIBS®
LIVE WITH HANSEL
AND GRETEL

The following is a/an _____ interview to be read aloud by
                ADJECTIVE

three _____ :
    PLURAL NOUN

Host: Welcome to *Fairy Tale Forum*. We're here live with the _____
                                                  ADJECTIVE

    Hansel and Gretel. Gretel, tell us what happened.

Gretel: Well, our _____ stepmother kept taking us into the
               ADJECTIVE

    woods so we'd get lost.

Hansel: But I left a trail of _____ so we could find our way back.
                      PLURAL NOUN

Host: But then something unexpected happened, right?

Gretel: Yes. We found a house made entirely of candy _____.
                                     PLURAL NOUN

Hansel: And we were so _____ that we started to eat it. But
                   ADJECTIVE

    then a witch popped out and put me in a/an _____.
                                     NOUN

Host: Oh, my _____! How did you escape?
           PLURAL NOUN

Hansel: Gretel pushed the witch into a/an _____ and
                           NOUN

    we ran home.

Host: What a/an _____ story. Viewers, join us next time when
            ADJECTIVE

    we find out if Prince Charming is secretly dating _____.
                                        CELEBRITY

From HAPPILY EVER MAD LIBS®. Copyright © 2010 by Price Stern Sloan,
a division of Penguin Young Readers Group, 345 Hudson Street, New York, NY 10014.

MAD LIBS® is fun to play with friends, but you can also play it by yourself! To begin with, DO NOT look at the story on the page below. Fill in the blanks on this page with the words called for. Then, using the words you have selected, fill in the blank spaces in the story.

Now you've created your own hilarious MAD LIBS® game!

THE WOLF'S SIDE OF THE STORY

ADJECTIVE _____

VERB ENDING IN "ING" _____

ADJECTIVE _____

NOUN _____

PART OF THE BODY (PLURAL) _____

PLURAL NOUN _____

NOUN _____

NOUN _____

PLURAL NOUN _____

PART OF THE BODY (PLURAL) _____

ADJECTIVE _____

NOUN _____

ADJECTIVE _____

ADJECTIVE _____

MAD LIBS®
THE WOLF'S SIDE
OF THE STORY

I am the big, _____ wolf. You may have heard the lies
          ADJECTIVE

Little Red _____ Hood has told about me. But now it's my
       VERB ENDING IN "ING"

turn to tell you the truth. One day Little Red Riding Hood was on her

way to visit her _____ grandmother. But I happened to get
              ADJECTIVE

there first. I knocked, but there was no answer. Then I remembered it

was Wednesday and Grandma would be at her weekly _____
                                                   NOUN

game. I'd been on my _____ all day, so I decided to let
                  PART OF THE BODY (PLURAL)

myself in to take a nap. It was freezing in the house, so I slipped into

one of Grandma's _____ and fell into a deep _____.
               PLURAL NOUN   NOUN

I was awakened by Little Red Riding _____ shouting at me,
                                      NOUN

saying insulting things like, "What big _____ you have!" and
                                     PLURAL NOUN

"What big _____ you have." Offended, I got up and
       PART OF THE BODY (PLURAL)

left. Believe me, that's the _____ truth and nothing but
                          ADJECTIVE

the _____. So, you see, I'm not the _____
        NOUN   ADJECTIVE

fiend Little Red makes me out to be. I'm the real victim in this

_____ tale!
     ADJECTIVE

MAD LIBS® is fun to play with friends, but you can also play it by yourself! To begin with, DO NOT look at the story on the page below. Fill in the blanks on this page with the words called for. Then, using the words you have selected, fill in the blank spaces in the story.

Now you've created your own hilarious MAD LIBS® game!

CASTLE FOR SALE

OCCUPATION _____

ADJECTIVE _____

ADJECTIVE _____

PERSON IN ROOM (MALE) _____

ADJECTIVE _____

ADJECTIVE _____

A PLACE _____

ADJECTIVE _____

PART OF THE BODY _____

PART OF THE BODY _____

PLURAL NOUN _____

NOUN _____

ADVERB _____

NOUN _____

VERB _____

ADJECTIVE _____

PLURAL NOUN _____

PLURAL NOUN _____

ADJECTIVE _____

NUMBER _____

MAD LIBS®

CASTLE FOR SALE

Are you a king, queen, or _____ looking for that perfectly
                          OCCUPATION

_____ new home? Then have we got a/an _____
ADJECTIVE   ADJECTIVE

place for you! King _____'s _____ castle
                   PERSON IN ROOM (MALE)   ADJECTIVE

has just come on the market! Originally built in the _____
                                                      ADJECTIVE

Ages, this lakefront wonder has towers that rise high above (the)

_____ and a/an _____ view that will take your
A PLACE   ADJECTIVE

_____ away. In each and every room of this 25,000 square-
PART OF THE BODY

_____ masterpiece, there are magnificent stained glass
PART OF THE BODY

_____ and splendid Gothic _____-burning
PLURAL NOUN   NOUN

fireplaces. There's also a chef's state-of-the-art, _____
                                                     ADVERB

modern _____ for those who love to _____.
        NOUN   VERB

For security and _____ privacy, there is also a moat filled
                  ADJECTIVE

with _____ and a drawbridge to keep out unwanted
      PLURAL NOUN

_____. Take advantage of the collapse in the castle
PLURAL NOUN

market and make a/an _____ offer on this treasure. The
                      ADJECTIVE

asking price is a ridiculously low _____ dollars.
                                    NUMBER

From HAPPILY EVER MAD LIBS®. Copyright © 2010 by Price Stern Sloan,
a division of Penguin Young Readers Group, 345 Hudson Street, New York, NY 10014.

MAD LIBS® is fun to play with friends, but you can also play it by yourself! To begin with, DO NOT look at the story on the page below. Fill in the blanks on this page with the words called for. Then, using the words you have selected, fill in the blank spaces in the story.

Now you've created your own hilarious MAD LIBS® game!

CINDERELLA

ADJECTIVE _____

ADJECTIVE _____

ADJECTIVE _____

PART OF THE BODY _____

NOUN _____

ADJECTIVE _____

NOUN _____

NOUN _____

NOUN _____

NOUN _____

PLURAL NOUN _____

PERSON IN ROOM (MALE) _____

PLURAL NOUN _____

PART OF THE BODY _____

ADVERB _____

MAD LIBS®

CINDERELLA

There once was a/an _____ young girl named Cinderella
                          ADJECTIVE

who lived with her _____ stepmother and two
                        ADJECTIVE

_____ stepsisters. She waited on them hand and
ADJECTIVE

_____, but they treated her like a/an _____.
PART OF THE BODY   NOUN

Cinderella heard about a ball the prince was throwing, but she

didn't have a/an _____ gown to wear. Then, out of the
                     ADJECTIVE

clear, blue _____, her fairy _____-mother appeared
                 NOUN   NOUN

and waved her magic _____. Cinderella's ragged clothes
                          NOUN

turned into a beautiful _____, and her worn work shoes
                              NOUN

became a pair of glass _____. Cinderella went to the ball
                            PLURAL NOUN

and danced with Prince _____, who fell madly in love
                         PERSON IN ROOM (MALE)

with her. But at the stroke of midnight she had to flee, losing one of

her glass _____. The prince traveled throughout the
              PLURAL NOUN

kingdom, trying the slipper on the _____ of every young
                                        PART OF THE BODY

girl, but, of course, it fit only one—Cinderella! The two were soon

married and lived _____ ever after.
                        ADVERB

From HAPPILY EVER MAD LIBS®. Copyright © 2010 by Price Stern Sloan,
a division of Penguin Young Readers Group, 345 Hudson Street, New York, NY 10014.

MAD LIBS® is fun to play with friends, but you can also play it by yourself! To begin with, DO NOT look at the story on the page below. Fill in the blanks on this page with the words called for. Then, using the words you have selected, fill in the blank spaces in the story.

Now you've created your own hilarious MAD LIBS® game!

PRINCESS SEEKING FAIRY GODMOTHER

ADJECTIVE _____

PERSON IN ROOM (FEMALE) _____

ADJECTIVE _____

ADJECTIVE _____

NUMBER _____

ADJECTIVE _____

PLURAL NOUN_____

NOUN _____

PLURAL NOUN_____

PLURAL NOUN_____

PLURAL NOUN_____

PLURAL NOUN_____

VERB ENDING IN "ING"_____

ADJECTIVE _____

PLURAL NOUN_____

PLURAL NOUN_____

PART OF THE BODY (PLURAL) _____

ADVERB _____

MAD LIBS®
PRINCESS SEEKING FAIRY GODMOTHER

Wanted: One _____ godmother needed immediately for
 ADJECTIVE

_____, a very _____ young princess
PERSON IN ROOM (FEMALE)   ADJECTIVE

with a/an _____ personality. Applicant must have
          ADJECTIVE

at least _____ years of _____ experience
         NUMBER   ADJECTIVE

helping princesses or other royal _____ live up to their
                                  PLURAL NOUN

_____ and making their _____ come
NOUN   PLURAL NOUN

true. The ideal candidate should be able to turn pumpkins into

_____ and mice into _____ who are
PLURAL NOUN   PLURAL NOUN

capable of pulling oversized _____. Since the princess
                             PLURAL NOUN

enjoys ballroom _____ with _____
                VERB ENDING IN "ING"   ADJECTIVE

princes, expertise in waltzes, polkas, and _____ is a
                                           PLURAL NOUN

must. Salary will be paid in golden _____—as many as
                                    PLURAL NOUN

you can carry in your _____. Please apply as
                      PART OF THE BODY (PLURAL)

_____ as possible!
ADVERB

MAD LIBS® is fun to play with friends, but you can also play it by yourself! To begin with, DO NOT look at the story on the page below. Fill in the blanks on this page with the words called for. Then, using the words you have selected, fill in the blank spaces in the story.

Now you've created your own hilarious MAD LIBS® game!

FROM A SPELL BOOK
FOR WICKED QUEENS

ADJECTIVE _____

ADJECTIVE _____

ADJECTIVE _____

ADJECTIVE _____

TYPE OF LIQUID _____

NOUN _____

NUMBER _____

PART OF THE BODY _____

NUMBER _____

ADJECTIVE _____

PART OF THE BODY _____

NOUN _____

NOUN _____

ADJECTIVE _____

ADJECTIVE _____

ADJECTIVE _____

ADJECTIVE _____

MAD LIBS®
FROM A SPELL BOOK
FOR WICKED QUEENS

Need to make a/an _____ princess fall into a deep,
                        ADJECTIVE

_____ sleep? Here is a recipe that will bring incredibly
ADJECTIVE

_____ results. First, put a large _____
ADJECTIVE   ADJECTIVE

cauldron, filled to the brim with _____, on an open
                                   TYPE OF LIQUID

_____ and heat to _____ degrees. When it
NOUN   NUMBER

begins to boil, add a/an _____ from a newt and
                         PART OF THE BODY

_____ freshly caught _____ lizards. Mash them
NUMBER   ADJECTIVE

up well and mix with the _____ of a toad and the
                          PART OF THE BODY

_____ of a small, furry _____. Once again,
NOUN   NOUN

bring to a/an _____ boil. Now you can offer the brew to
              ADJECTIVE

any unsuspecting _____ princess. They fall for it every
                 ADJECTIVE

time. But beware: No matter how strong the _____
                                            ADJECTIVE

potion is, true love will reverse its _____ spell
                                       ADJECTIVE

every time!

MAD LIBS® is fun to play with friends, but you can also play it by yourself! To begin with, DO NOT look at the story on the page below. Fill in the blanks on this page with the words called for. Then, using the words you have selected, fill in the blank spaces in the story.

Now you've created your own hilarious MAD LIBS® game!

THE THREE BILLY GOATS GRUFF

ADJECTIVE _____

ADJECTIVE _____

ADJECTIVE _____

NOUN _____

VERB _____

NOUN _____

NOUN _____

ADJECTIVE _____

NOUN _____

ADVERB _____

EXCLAMATION _____

NOUN _____

NOUN _____

MAD LIBS®
THE THREE
BILLY GOATS GRUFF

Once there were three _____ billy goats with the last name
ADJECTIVE

of Gruff. They wanted to cross a river to eat the _____
ADJECTIVE

grass on the other side. But the bridge was guarded by a fearsome,

_____ troll who devoured any _____ who
ADJECTIVE   NOUN

tried to cross it. When the first and littlest billy goat started to

_____ over the bridge, the terrifying _____
VERB   NOUN

shouted, "I'm going to eat you!" Thinking fast on his _____,
NOUN

the billy goat said, "Wait, I have a brother who is bigger and more

_____ than I am. You can eat him." So the troll waited
ADJECTIVE

for the next billy _____. When he appeared, the same
NOUN

thing happened. So the troll waited _____ for the third
ADVERB

and biggest billy goat. This time the troll jumped out and cried,

"_____! I am going to eat you!" But the biggest billy goat
EXCLAMATION

simply lifted the troll with his horns and knocked him into the raging

_____ below. From then on, the billy goats feasted in the
NOUN

fields on the other side of the _____ to their hearts' content.
NOUN

From HAPPILY EVER MAD LIBS®. Copyright © 2010 by Price Stern Sloan,
a division of Penguin Young Readers Group, 345 Hudson Street, New York, NY 10014.

MAD LIBS® is fun to play with friends, but you can also play it by yourself! To begin with, DO NOT look at the story on the page below. Fill in the blanks on this page with the words called for. Then, using the words you have selected, fill in the blank spaces in the story.

Now you've created your own hilarious MAD LIBS® game!

RECIPE FOR THE
BEST PORRIDGE EVER

PERSON IN ROOM (FEMALE) _____

PLURAL NOUN_____

ADJECTIVE _____

NOUN _____

ADJECTIVE _____

ADJECTIVE _____

PLURAL NOUN_____

ADJECTIVE _____

PLURAL NOUN_____

NUMBER _____

NOUN _____

ADJECTIVE _____

PLURAL NOUN_____

ADJECTIVE _____

ADJECTIVE _____

NOUN _____

PLURAL NOUN_____

MAD LIBS®
RECIPE FOR THE
BEST PORRIDGE EVER

Hi. I'm _____, but you probably know me as
PERSON IN ROOM (FEMALE)

Mama Bear from *Goldilocks and the Three* _____.
PLURAL NOUN

I'm here to tell you about making incredibly _____
ADJECTIVE

porridge. Lots of folks say that eating my porridge is even

better than eating a juicy sirloin _____. To make
NOUN

really _____ porridge, you start by filling a/an
ADJECTIVE

_____ pot with water. Then add two cups of oats, a
ADJECTIVE

few chopped _____, and plenty of _____
PLURAL NOUN   ADJECTIVE

_____. Place the pot on the stove for _____
PLURAL NOUN   NUMBER

hours. Stir with a/an _____ so it will be nice and
NOUN

_____. This recipe should amply serve three bears or
ADJECTIVE

fifty-three _____. Now, some like it _____,
PLURAL NOUN   ADJECTIVE

some like it _____, and some like it just right. And, by
ADJECTIVE

the way, unless you plan to share this porridge, be on the lookout for

_____-stealing girls named Goldi-_____.
NOUN   PLURAL NOUN

From HAPPILY EVER MAD LIBS®. Copyright © 2010 by Price Stern Sloan,
a division of Penguin Young Readers Group, 345 Hudson Street, New York, NY 10014.

MAD LIBS® is fun to play with friends, but you can also play it by yourself! To begin with, DO NOT look at the story on the page below. Fill in the blanks on this page with the words called for. Then, using the words you have selected, fill in the blank spaces in the story.

Now you've created your own hilarious MAD LIBS® game!

RUMPELSTILTSKIN

OCCUPATION _____

ADJECTIVE _____

NOUN _____

ADJECTIVE _____

PART OF THE BODY _____

PLURAL NOUN _____

NOUN _____

NOUN _____

ADVERB _____

ADJECTIVE _____

PART OF THE BODY (PLURAL) _____

ADJECTIVE _____

RUMPELSTILTSKIN

There once was a greedy _____ who said that his daughter
　　　　　　　　　　　　　　　OCCUPATION

could spin straw into gold. The _____ king put the girl in a
　　　　　　　　　　　　　　　　ADJECTIVE

room filled with straw and gave her until the _____ rose to
　　　　　　　　　　　　　　　　　　　　　　　NOUN

prove herself. She knew she wasn't capable of such a feat, but at

midnight, a/an _____ man appeared. "I'll turn the straw into
　　　　　　　　ADJECTIVE

gold if you give me the necklace around your _____," he
　　　　　　　　　　　　　　　　　　　　　　PART OF THE BODY

said. She did, and the room filled with golden _____. The
　　　　　　　　　　　　　　　　　　　　　　PLURAL NOUN

same thing happened the next night and cost the girl her

_____. On the third night, she had nothing to offer. "In
NOUN

that case," he said, "your firstborn _____ will be mine." She
　　　　　　　　　　　　　　　　　NOUN

_____ agreed. But when the girl was happily married to
ADVERB

the king and they had a baby, the little man reappeared. He said, "If you

can guess my name, I will release you from your _____
　　　　　　　　　　　　　　　　　　　　　　　　ADJECTIVE

promise." "Rumpelstiltskin," the queen guessed. The little man

couldn't believe his _____. She was right! So
　　　　　　　　　　PART OF THE BODY (PLURAL)

Rumpelstiltskin raced out of the castle in a/an _____ rage.
　　　　　　　　　　　　　　　　　　　　　　　ADJECTIVE

MAD LIBS® is fun to play with friends, but you can also play it by yourself! To begin with, DO NOT look at the story on the page below. Fill in the blanks on this page with the words called for. Then, using the words you have selected, fill in the blank spaces in the story.

Now you've created your own hilarious MAD LIBS® game!

HOW TO BE A PRINCESS

PART OF THE BODY _____

ADJECTIVE _____

ADJECTIVE _____

PLURAL NOUN _____

ADJECTIVE _____

ADJECTIVE _____

NOUN _____

ADVERB _____

ADJECTIVE _____

ADJECTIVE _____

ADJECTIVE _____

VERB ENDING IN "ING" _____

ADJECTIVE _____

ADJECTIVE _____

ADVERB _____

MAD LIBS®
HOW TO BE A PRINCESSS

It is difficult not to envy a young woman who has everything her

_____ desires. But history shows it isn't easy being a
PART OF THE BODY

princess. You have to maintain _____ standards and abide
ADJECTIVE

by _____ rules. For example:
ADJECTIVE

• A princess should always be kind to, and understanding of, her

royal _____. A princess knows that a/an _____
PLURAL NOUN   ADJECTIVE

smile is preferable to a/an _____ frown.
ADJECTIVE

• A princess should be a patron of the arts, well-versed in classical

_____, and _____ familiar with
NOUN   ADVERB

_____ authors and their _____ works.
ADJECTIVE   ADJECTIVE

• A princess should never make a/an _____ decision. She
ADJECTIVE

should always think before _____. And when she
VERB ENDING IN "ING"

does speak, she should be articulate and, if possible, very

_____.
ADJECTIVE

• And, of course, a princess must be prepared to marry a/an

_____ prince and live _____ ever after.
ADJECTIVE   ADVERB

MAD LIBS® is fun to play with friends, but you can also play it by yourself! To begin with, DO NOT look at the story on the page below. Fill in the blanks on this page with the words called for. Then, using the words you have selected, fill in the blank spaces in the story.

Now you've created your own hilarious MAD LIBS® game!

MAGICAL WEDDING INVITATION

PERSON IN ROOM (FEMALE) _____

PERSON IN ROOM (MALE) _____

ADJECTIVE _____

ADJECTIVE _____

CELEBRITY (FEMALE) _____

PLURAL NOUN _____

CELEBRITY (MALE) _____

A PLACE _____

ADJECTIVE _____

ARTICLE OF CLOTHING (PLURAL) _____

NOUN _____

PLURAL NOUN _____

ADJECTIVE _____

PERSON IN ROOM _____

PLURAL NOUN _____

ADJECTIVE _____

MAD LIBS®
MAGICAL WEDDING INVITATION

You are hereby cordially invited by Queen _____
_{PERSON IN ROOM (FEMALE)}

and King _____ to a most _____ event—
_{PERSON IN ROOM (MALE)}   _{ADJECTIVE}

the marriage of Sleeping Beauty to the most _____ Prince
_{ADJECTIVE}

Charming. The bride will be attended by her maid of honor,

_____, and her seven _____, while
_{CELEBRITY (FEMALE)}   _{PLURAL NOUN}

_____ is the best man. The ceremony will take
_{CELEBRITY (MALE)}

place in the enchanted forest near (the) _____. All female
_{A PLACE}

guests are encouraged to wear _____ dresses, while for
_{ADJECTIVE}

men, fancy _____ are recommended. The
_{ARTICLE OF CLOTHING (PLURAL)}

dinner menu will include roast _____ and sweet
_{NOUN}

_____ for dessert. The band, _____,
_{PLURAL NOUN}   _{ADJECTIVE}

_____ and the _____, will provide music
_{PERSON IN ROOM}   _{PLURAL NOUN}

for dancing. Please RSVP at your earliest convenience. A/An

_____ time is guaranteed for all.
_{ADJECTIVE}

MAD LIBS® is fun to play with friends, but you can also play it by yourself! To begin with, DO NOT look at the story on the page below. Fill in the blanks on this page with the words called for. Then, using the words you have selected, fill in the blank spaces in the story.

Now you've created your own hilarious MAD LIBS® game!

SNOW WHITE AT THE SEVEN DWARFS' COTTAGE

ADJECTIVE _____

PERSON IN ROOM (FEMALE) _____

A PLACE _____

ADJECTIVE _____

PLURAL NOUN _____

PLURAL NOUN _____

ADJECTIVE _____

PLURAL NOUN _____

PLURAL NOUN _____

NOUN _____

PERSON IN ROOM _____

PERSON IN ROOM _____

ADJECTIVE _____

ADJECTIVE _____

A PLACE _____

OCCUPATION _____

MAD LIBS®
SNOW WHITE AT THE
SEVEN DWARFS' COTTAGE

My name is Snow White, and I am hiding from my _____
ADJECTIVE

stepmother, _____, at the Seven Dwarfs' cottage
PERSON IN ROOM (FEMALE)

in (the) _____. It is a/an _____ little place
A PLACE   ADJECTIVE

with a roof made of _____. Since the dwarfs are letting
PLURAL NOUN

me stay here, I help out by dusting the _____, cooking
PLURAL NOUN

_____ dinners, and washing their _____.
ADJECTIVE   PLURAL NOUN

The dwarfs and I have become really close _____ and
PLURAL NOUN

enjoy one another's _____ very much. Their names
NOUN

are Sleepy, Happy, _____, _____,
PERSON IN ROOM   PERSON IN ROOM

Sneezy, _____, and Doc. The dwarfs and I share many
ADJECTIVE

_____ interests. We especially like to sing, "Hi ho,
ADJECTIVE

hi ho, it's off to (the) _____ we go!" Oh, sorry,
A PLACE

have to run now. There's a sweet, old _____ at the
OCCUPATION

door selling apples.

From HAPPILY EVER MAD LIBS®. Copyright © 2010 by Price Stern Sloan,
a division of Penguin Young Readers Group, 345 Hudson Street, New York, NY 10014.

MAD LIBS® is fun to play with friends, but you can also play it by yourself! To begin with, DO NOT look at the story on the page below. Fill in the blanks on this page with the words called for. Then, using the words you have selected, fill in the blank spaces in the story.

Now you've created your own hilarious MAD LIBS® game!

THE GINGERBREAD MAN'S EXERCISE ROUTINE

VERB _____

SAME VERB _____

NOUN _____

ADJECTIVE _____

PLURAL NOUN _____

ADJECTIVE _____

ADVERB _____

ADJECTIVE _____

NOUN _____

PART OF THE BODY (PLURAL) _____

NUMBER _____

NOUN _____

PART OF THE BODY _____

VERB _____

PART OF THE BODY _____

NOUN _____

ADJECTIVE _____

NOUN _____

PLURAL NOUN _____

MAD LIBS®
THE GINGERBREAD MAN'S EXERCISE ROUTINE

_____, _____ as fast as you can. You can't
　　　VERB　　　　　　SAME VERB

catch me—I'm the Gingerbread _____! And I'm known
　　　　　　　　　　　　　　　　　NOUN

for running at _____ speeds to keep people and
　　　　　　　　ADJECTIVE

_____ from trying to eat me. I guess it's because I smell
PLURAL NOUN

so _____. But I have to work _____ hard to
　　ADJECTIVE　　　　　　　　　　　　　ADVERB

stay in _____ shape. I start my day when the
　　　　ADJECTIVE

_____ comes up. I warm up by stretching to loosen my
　　NOUN

_____ for approximately _____ minutes.
PART OF THE BODY (PLURAL)　　　　　　NUMBER

For weight lifting exercises, I lift a candy _____ over
　　　　　　　　　　　　　　　　　　　　　　　NOUN

my head to strengthen my abs and _____. I do
　　　　　　　　　　　　　　　　PART OF THE BODY

_____-ups to develop strength in my _____.
　VERB　　　　　　　　　　　　　　　　　　PART OF THE BODY

And I always eat a healthy breakfast that includes lots of shredded

_____. This routine may sound a little _____,
　NOUN　　　　　　　　　　　　　　　　　　　　　ADJECTIVE

but it can really make you feel as fit as a/an _____.
　　　　　　　　　　　　　　　　　　　　　NOUN

And you'll never have to worry about getting eaten by hungry

_____!
PLURAL NOUN

From HAPPILY EVER MAD LIBS®. Copyright © 2010 by Price Stern Sloan,
a division of Penguin Young Readers Group, 345 Hudson Street, New York, NY 10014.

MAD LIBS® is fun to play with friends, but you can also play it by yourself! To begin with, DO NOT look at the story on the page below. Fill in the blanks on this page with the words called for. Then, using the words you have selected, fill in the blank spaces in the story.

Now you've created your own hilarious MAD LIBS® game!

UNDER THE SEA WITH THE LITTLE MERMAID

PLURAL NOUN _____

ADJECTIVE _____

ADJECTIVE _____

PLURAL NOUN _____

PERSON IN ROOM (MALE) _____

NOUN _____

PLURAL NOUN _____

NOUN _____

PLURAL NOUN _____

VERB _____

PART OF THE BODY (PLURAL) _____

VERB _____

PLURAL NOUN _____

ADJECTIVE _____

PLURAL NOUN _____

PART OF THE BODY (PLURAL) _____

OCCUPATION _____

ADVERB _____

NOUN _____

MAD LIBS®
UNDER THE SEA WITH THE LITTLE MERMAID

Life under the sea is full of wonder and _____
PLURAL NOUN

—especially when you're a mermaid and a/an _____
ADJECTIVE

underwater princess like me! I live on the ocean floor in a/an

_____ castle made of coral _____. My dad
ADJECTIVE   PLURAL NOUN

is King _____, ruler of the entire _____.
PERSON IN ROOM (MALE)   NOUN

My friends are fish, dolphins, and underwater _____.
PLURAL NOUN

We spend our days exploring _____ reefs and searching
NOUN

for sunken _____. Sometimes I wonder what it would
PLURAL NOUN

be like to _____ on land. I've heard that people there
VERB

have _____ instead of fins. And that they
PART OF THE BODY (PLURAL)

_____ around from place to place in motorized
VERB

_____ and wear _____ _____
PLURAL NOUN   ADJECTIVE   PLURAL NOUN

on their _____. Someday I hope to visit this
PART OF THE BODY (PLURAL)

place so I can meet a handsome _____ and fall
OCCUPATION

_____ in love. That would be a mermaid's
ADVERB

_____ come true!
NOUN

From HAPPILY EVER MAD LIBS®. Copyright © 2010 by Price Stern Sloan,
a division of Penguin Young Readers Group, 345 Hudson Street, New York, NY 10014.

MAD LIBS® is fun to play with friends, but you can also play it by yourself! To begin with, DO NOT look at the story on the page below. Fill in the blanks on this page with the words called for. Then, using the words you have selected, fill in the blank spaces in the story.

Now you've created your own hilarious MAD LIBS® game!

RAPUNZEL'S HAIR TIPS

ADJECTIVE _____

NOUN _____

PLURAL NOUN_____

PLURAL NOUN_____

NOUN _____

NUMBER _____

PLURAL NOUN_____

ADJECTIVE _____

ADJECTIVE _____

NOUN _____

NUMBER _____

PART OF THE BODY _____

ADJECTIVE _____

PERSON IN ROOM (MALE) _____

ADJECTIVE _____

MAD LIBS®

RAPUNZEL'S HAIR TIPS

Hi, my dears. Rapunzel here. As you may know, I'm famous for my

long and _____ hair. How do I maintain it? Here are some
          ADJECTIVE

tips that will help you get a beautiful _____ just like mine:
                                            NOUN

• Use shampoo made from all-natural _____ and
                                          PLURAL NOUN

   _____.
   PLURAL NOUN

• Be sure to groom your hair with a fine-tooth _____ for
                                                    NOUN

   _____ hours a day.
   NUMBER

• Eat plenty of fresh _____: The natural oils will give your
                        PLURAL NOUN

   hair a/an _____ sheen and _____ body.
              ADJECTIVE   ADJECTIVE

• Wash your _____ no more than _____ times a
                NOUN   NUMBER

   day. Otherwise, it will get dry and you may look like you stuck your

   _____ in a light socket.
   PART OF THE BODY

Follow these _____ tips and Prince _____ will
                ADJECTIVE   PERSON IN ROOM (MALE)

be able to climb up your hair and rescue you if you should happen

to be imprisoned in a/an _____ tower!
                            ADJECTIVE

MAD LIBS® is fun to play with friends, but you can also play it by yourself! To begin with, DO NOT look at the story on the page below. Fill in the blanks on this page with the words called for. Then, using the words you have selected, fill in the blank spaces in the story.

Now you've created your own hilarious MAD LIBS® game!

A NEW FAIRY TALE

ADJECTIVE _____

PERSON IN ROOM (FEMALE) _____

NOUN _____

A PLACE_____

ADJECTIVE _____

PART OF THE BODY _____

ADJECTIVE _____

ADJECTIVE _____

ADJECTIVE _____

NOUN _____

NOUN _____

NOUN _____

VERB _____

PLURAL NOUN_____

NOUN _____

ADJECTIVE _____

MAD LIBS®

A NEW FAIRY TALE

Once upon a time, there lived a/an _____, young
                                            ADJECTIVE

girl named _____ who lived in a little
            PERSON IN ROOM (FEMALE)

wooden _____ by (the) _____. She was
          NOUN   A PLACE

a/an _____ child, always willing to lend a/an
          ADJECTIVE

_____ to the _____ villagers. She was small
PART OF THE BODY   ADJECTIVE

and _____ but worked very hard. Then, one day, she
        ADJECTIVE

happened upon a/an _____ frog. To her surprise, this little
                        ADJECTIVE

slimy _____ could talk! In a deep, croaky voice, it said,
          NOUN

"I will grant you three wishes, but then you must give me a/an

_____ on the lips." She agreed. And for her first wish, she
    NOUN

asked for a new _____ for her parents to live in. For her
                    NOUN

second, she wished to be able to _____ like a bird. For her
                                        VERB

final wish, she asked for all the _____ in the world! And it
                                    PLURAL NOUN

all came to pass just as the frog said. The girl kissed the frog and he

suddenly turned into a handsome, young _____. She
                                            NOUN

couldn't believe her _____ luck!
                          ADJECTIVE

From HAPPILY EVER MAD LIBS®. Copyright © 2010 by Price Stern Sloan,
a division of Penguin Young Readers Group, 345 Hudson Street, New York, NY 10014.

MAD LIBS® is fun to play with friends, but you can also play it by yourself! To begin with, DO NOT look at the story on the page below. Fill in the blanks on this page with the words called for. Then, using the words you have selected, fill in the blank spaces in the story.

Now you've created your own hilarious MAD LIBS® game!

PINOCCHIO'S DIARY

NOUN _____

ADJECTIVE _____

NOUN _____

ADJECTIVE _____

NOUN _____

NOUN _____

PERSON IN ROOM (MALE) _____

ADJECTIVE _____

ADJECTIVE _____

ADVERB _____

NOUN _____

PART OF THE BODY (PLURAL) _____

PART OF THE BODY _____

NUMBER _____

NOUN _____

MAD LIBS®

PINOCCHIO'S DIARY

6:20 AM: Woke up this morning, looked at my face in the

_____, and I was still nothing but a/an _____
NOUN   ADJECTIVE

puppet carved out of _____. Depressed, went back to sleep.
                            NOUN

6:50 AM: Awakened by a/an _____ fairy. She said that if I
                                    ADJECTIVE

want to become a real _____, I must have a conscience.
                              NOUN

Then she disappeared into thin _____.
                                        NOUN

7:12 AM: A cricket named _____ visited me. He
                                PERSON IN ROOM (MALE)

said that a boy with a good conscience can tell right from

_____, and he always speaks the _____ truth. He
    ADJECTIVE   ADJECTIVE

added that if I lie, it will become _____ apparent to everyone.
                                            ADVERB

7:30 AM: Excited, I woke up my dad, Geppetto, and told him that I

had become a real _____, just like he always wanted.
                          NOUN

Geppetto's _____ filled with tears.
              PART OF THE BODY (PLURAL)

8:30 AM: Geppetto asked if I would like to go to school. I said yes.

Suddenly my _____ grew _____ inches. I took a
                PART OF THE BODY   NUMBER

solemn _____ never to lie again.
            NOUN

From HAPPILY EVER MAD LIBS®. Copyright © 2010 by Price Stern Sloan,
a division of Penguin Young Readers Group, 345 Hudson Street, New York, NY 10014.

MAD LIBS® is fun to play with friends, but you can also play it by yourself! To begin with, DO NOT look at the story on the page below. Fill in the blanks on this page with the words called for. Then, using the words you have selected, fill in the blank spaces in the story.

Now you've created your own hilarious MAD LIBS® game!

MAGIC WAND FOR SALE

OCCUPATION _____

NOUN _____

PLURAL NOUN _____

PLURAL NOUN _____

PLURAL NOUN _____

PERSON IN ROOM (MALE) _____

PLURAL NOUN _____

PLURAL NOUN _____

ADJECTIVE _____

NUMBER _____

PLURAL NOUN _____

ADJECTIVE _____

ADJECTIVE _____

PLURAL NOUN _____

MAD LIBS®

MAGIC WAND FOR SALE

Are you a wizard, a fairy godmother, or a/an _____ looking

OCCUPATION

for a magic _____ that can do it all? Do you need to turn

NOUN

frogs into _____ or make _____ fly or have an

PLURAL NOUN   PLURAL NOUN

evil witch vanish into a puff of smoke? Well, look no further! This is

the wand that can do anything! That's right—the Wandinator 2000 is

here! Handcrafted from the finest _____, this is the

PLURAL NOUN

same wand that the famous wizard _____ uses.

PERSON IN ROOM (MALE)

With the Wandinator 2000, you, too, can change a pile of worthless

_____ into valuable _____. Tired of wands that

PLURAL NOUN   PLURAL NOUN

are _____ and wear out too fast? The Wandinator 2000 is

ADJECTIVE

guaranteed to last _____ years or your _____

NUMBER   PLURAL NOUN

back! Act now and get a free _____ carrying case. Don't

ADJECTIVE

miss this _____ opportunity. Buy it now! Gold, silver,

ADJECTIVE

_____, and credit cards accepted.

PLURAL NOUN

MAD LIBS® is fun to play with friends, but you can also play it by yourself! To begin with, DO NOT look at the story on the page below. Fill in the blanks on this page with the words called for. Then, using the words you have selected, fill in the blank spaces in the story.

Now you've created your own hilarious MAD LIBS® game!

SO YOU WANT TO BE A VILLAIN?

ADJECTIVE _____

NOUN _____

PLURAL NOUN _____

ADJECTIVE _____

PERSON IN ROOM _____

PERSON IN ROOM _____

NOUN _____

ADJECTIVE _____

PLURAL NOUN _____

PERSON IN ROOM _____

CELEBRITY _____

PLURAL NOUN _____

OCCUPATION (PLURAL) _____

ADJECTIVE _____

ADJECTIVE _____

ADJECTIVE _____

MAD LIBS®
SO YOU WANT
TO BE A VILLAIN?

It is not easy being a/an _____ villain in a sea of fairy
                        ADJECTIVE

_____-mothers, magical _____, and
NOUN   PLURAL NOUN

_____ princes and princesses. To be a really
ADJECTIVE

successful villain like Count _____ or _____
                            PERSON IN ROOM   PERSON IN ROOM

the Wicked _____ will take practice and the right tools.
           NOUN

First, you'll need a really _____ laugh, since you have to
                           ADJECTIVE

cackle alongside the most evil witches and horrible _____.
                                                    PLURAL NOUN

It is also recommended that you hire some evil henchmen like

_____ or _____ to help you steal golden
PERSON IN ROOM   CELEBRITY

_____ or kidnap wealthy _____. And, of
PLURAL NOUN   OCCUPATION (PLURAL)

course, you'll need a place to hide out. A dark, _____ cave
                                                 ADJECTIVE

is good, but so are _____ alleys. Follow these directions
                    ADJECTIVE

and you will certainly become a really _____, world-
                                       ADJECTIVE

famous villain!

From HAPPILY EVER MAD LIBS®. Copyright © 2010 by Price Stern Sloan,
a division of Penguin Young Readers Group, 345 Hudson Street, New York, NY 10014.

MAD LIBS® is fun to play with friends, but you can also play it by yourself! To begin with, DO NOT look at the story on the page below. Fill in the blanks on this page with the words called for. Then, using the words you have selected, fill in the blank spaces in the story.

Now you've created your own hilarious MAD LIBS® game!

THE PRINCESS AND THE PEA

PERSON IN ROOM (MALE) _____

PERSON IN ROOM (FEMALE) _____

ADJECTIVE _____

ADJECTIVE _____

NOUN _____

NOUN _____

NOUN _____

ADJECTIVE _____

NOUN _____

ADJECTIVE _____

ADJECTIVE _____

ADVERB _____

A PLACE _____

MAD LIBS®
THE PRINCESS AND THE PEA

There once was a prince named _____. His
PERSON IN ROOM (MALE)

mother, Queen _____, summoned many princesses
PERSON IN ROOM (FEMALE)

to meet him. But none were _____ enough. Then one
ADJECTIVE

night, during a/an _____ storm, the prince heard a loud
ADJECTIVE

knock at the _____. He opened it, and there stood a fair
NOUN

maiden, soaking wet but as beautiful as a summer's _____.
NOUN

It was love at first _____. The girl said she was a princess, but
NOUN

the queen was doubtful. Luckily, she had a way to make sure. She

took the girl to a/an _____ bedroom where she had piled
ADJECTIVE

mattress upon mattress until they almost reached the ceiling.

Underneath, she placed a tiny _____. If the young woman
NOUN

felt the pea through the mattresses, she was really a/an _____
ADJECTIVE

princess. Sure enough, the next morning, the maiden complained

that she was unable to sleep because the _____ bed was so
ADJECTIVE

uncomfortable. The prince married her and they lived _____
ADVERB

ever after in (the) _____.
A PLACE

This book is published by

PSS!
PRICE STERN SLOAN

whose other splendid titles include
such literary classics as